PRAISE FOR *40 WORDS* BY DAVE DEBLANDER

"If you are looking for a book to awaken your entrepreneurial spirit, give new meaning to your purpose and provide a blueprint for success, then you must read this book! Dave DeBlander will motivate and inspire you to reach higher and go farther in your personal and professional life."

~ MICHELLE PRINCE, best-selling author of *Winning In Life Now*

"What if you could extract the success secrets of 75 of the most successful people in America? What if you could distill their success down to just ONE word? And what if you could learn why and how that word helped them become phenomenally successful? Would that help you make more money, improve your relationships and be happier and healthier? I think so. And the good news is you don't have to spend a lifetime researching the subject. In this book, Dave DeBlander has done it for you. Put these 40 words to work for YOU today!"

~ HOWARD PARTRIDGE, President, Phenomenal Products, Inc.

"Discipline, Clarity, Energy, Humor...these are a few of my favorite words. And they are included in Dave's 40. I love this book! Inspiring stories culled from 75 influential people. Dave, thanks for this powerful, positive book!"

~ ELLEN ROHR, author, speaker, entrepreneur,
President, Bare Bones Biz

"Dave DeBlander is more than a great financial success story. With great investigative zeal, Dave found 40 words that have changed ultra successful peoples' lives. Learn today how to awaken the entrepreneurial spirit within you by studying these words, implementing these words and using them as a basis for your quantum leap to living a good life."

~ MARK EHRLICH, business strategist, coach and keynote speaker,
President, Financial Systems and Services

"I found your book refreshing and enjoyable. *40 Words* is a primer for the pursuit in the basics of the business arena. Your book integrates Heart, Soul, (God) and opportunity. Your book is an easy read and contains all the elements of the basics of business as well as the game of life."

~ WILLIAM J. ROBBINS, President and Senior Marketing Executive,
Robbins Marketing Group

"*40 Words* is a collection of effective steps toward achieving personal and professional excellence. Each chapter presents a unique lesson in paths to self-improvement. The reader is shown the value of a positive attitude and the awareness that we should not be satisfied to endure our current space in life if it is unfulfilling. The individual is encouraged to take further action: to be aggressive in the development of self-awareness and success."

~ NAN HARPER, past President, Florida Chapter
of the Women's Council of Realtors

"This is a book with forty powerful messages for the reader. As a small business owner and Escambia county Commissioner for many years, I found it to be very motivational. If these precepts are properly applied, it will benefit both your professional and personal life. I highly recommend the book."

~ WILSON ROBERTSON, Entrepreneur and Escambia County,
Florida, County Commissioner

"There are a lot of times in life where I feel I am taking the journey alone. After discovering Dave DeBlander's book *40 Words*, my insight on life's journey has changed. The book was so inspirational that I found myself being brought to tears throughout by his words of wisdom. From the moment I opened this book I found myself engulfed with inspiration that seemed to come straight from the author's heart. I felt like Dave was saying everything directly to me as if we were old friends talking over a fresh cup of coffee. In reading this book, I find the part I love most is feeling that someone actually believes in me. I can honestly say I feel important, motivated, and propelled towards making a difference in my life, and most of all I no longer feel I am taking this journey alone."

~ KRISTEN RAMOS, Administrative Assistant

40
WORDS

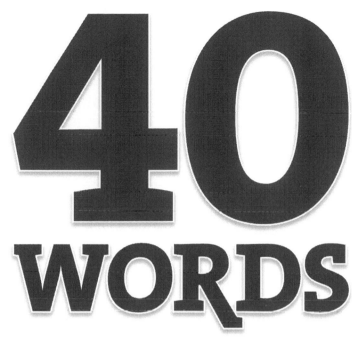

40 WORDS

{To Awaken The Entrepreneur Within}

by Dave DeBlander

Published by Dave DeBlander
Edited by Dan Madson
Cover and interior design by Josh Brigham of Redfin Design

ISBN-10: 0615505805 (Dave DeBlander)
ISBN-13: 978-0615505800 (Dave DeBlander)

This book is dedicated to my incredible family. I am blessed beyond measure to have a gorgeous, successful and tender-hearted wife without whom I never could have written this book. Kate is the wind beneath my wings. My life is now an absolute dream because I have the greatest daughter, son-in-law and grandchildren living just down the street. I would be remiss without thanking God who has blessed me beyond my wildest dreams.

CONTENTS

FOREWORD

On a recent trip to Florence, Italy, I stood before Michelangelo's famous sculpture of David. Like the rest of the visitors, I was astounded by the statue's beauty. The detailed craftsmanship of the 17-foot high monument is incomparable! Nearby, there are four other statues that Michelangelo never finished. In each of the four, parts of the faces and most of the bodies are incomplete. I had an eerie feeling there was a body inside each stone desperately trying to get out. When Michelangelo was asked how he could create such beautiful masterpieces, he said, "There are figures in each block of marble. They just need to be freed."

There is a giant inside each of you. Have you ever stopped to ponder what you could do with your life if you released that giant? Have you ever asked yourself, "Why can't I have it all? Why can't I be the best of the best in my field? Why can't I make an impact that will be felt for generations?" It's not necessarily about having more money or more things. Rather, it's about living your life to the fullest. It's about solving problems for yourself and your loved ones. It's about helping make the world a better place in which to live.

Ask a group of six-year-olds, "How many of you can sing or dance or draw?" Every hand will shoot up. Most kids would be ready to start singing, dancing and drawing right there! Ask a group of adults the same question and one or two hands may go up. What happened over the years? What squelched the desire to be creative and active? What doused the entrepreneurial spirit?

I would like you to accompany me on a great adventure. Together we are going to find the giant, that entrepreneurial spirit residing inside you. God filled each of you with creative urges, an essential element of entrepreneurship, and he expects you to live your life as he intended.

I would like to show you how to fan into flame the entrepreneurial spark that flickers inside of you.

It's possible you will need help to release the giant inside of you. This book can be part of the process. As you read *40 Words*, open your mind to the potential that you have to be great. The stories and messages in this book will inspire you and propel you toward success. You can have an exciting, fulfilling, significant life if you allow the giant inside of you to emerge.

INTRODUCTION

Enjoy each day! It's one of the principles by which I've lived my entire life. One of the reasons I wrote this book was to share ideas that can help change people's lives. Many entrepreneurs that I know live amazing, satisfying lives. I would love to see others change their lives from stress and pressure to satisfaction and success.

People become entrepreneurs after dreaming of developing business opportunities that will set them on pathways to success. They relish the ideas of financial freedom, independence, flexibility and realization of the American dream. For many, the American dream has turned into a nightmare of long hours at work and financial worries. For some, entrepreneurial success has become an all-consuming passion that leaves little time for enjoying life.

This book will help you understand success, enjoy the rewards of your work and balance your entrepreneurial passion with all your other responsibilities.

I've asked 75 successful businessmen and women to describe in one word what leads to success. My desire for each of you reading this book is to have an 'aha moment.' A moment where something clicks. A moment where you clarify a goal or commitment. A moment where you come to a new understanding about your purpose in life.

Andy Warhol once said that business is the highest form of art. In my business, I liken myself to the conductor of an orchestra. I see marketing as the string section. Operations is like the percussion section, and administration is like the brass section. When everything is in tune and playing together, it's a beautiful thing!

The American dream is alive and well! Why not stake your claim? Decide right now to be the best you can be. Rearrange your attitude; lean into the belief of your family, friends and mentors. Take massive action! Let the adventure begin.

By the way, I would love to hear about your 'aha moment.' When it happens, send me an email at dave@davedeblander.com.

Success

"Tell me in a word what it takes to be successful." I directed that statement at seventy-five of the most successful people I know. These men and women are some of the happiest, healthiest and most excited people on the planet. Over the past 16 years I've had the opportunity to interact with top achievers from my wife Kate's direct selling company. Many of them are entrepreneurial superstars who can light up a room upon entering. They have earned executive incomes, traveled the world and developed leaders of their own. Many of the 40 words featured in this book are gleaned from conversations I've had with these top businesswomen and their husbands. For those of you who are searching for answers to questions about what it takes to be successful, this book is a great place to start!

Saying that my personal journey in life has been unique and varied is an understatement. From high school basketball star to hippie to restaurant/ bakery owner to evangelist to business owner and writer, I've seen and done it all. Living in our dream home on Pensacola Beach, I'm able to manage my turnkey business, coach others to success and spend time with my wife. Our daughter, son-in-law and two grandchildren live nearby, so we are one big happy family. With our successes combined, my wife and I have been able to travel the world, live independent and fulfilling lives and help others achieve their dreams and goals.

When you examine *40 Words*, I believe you will discover what it takes to be successful in business and in life. It's possible you are determined, energetic and have a great work ethic but lack focus. You might have patience and persistence but lack passion. It's possible you're one step away from throwing in the towel. It's also possible that you're one step away from experiencing success like never before.

I believe three groups of people will benefit from this book:
1. Business owners and entrepreneurs who are stuck in a rut, unhappy and frustrated.
2. Business owners and entrepreneurs who are on the verge of great success but need to put the final piece of the puzzle in place.
3. Business owners who are already successful but lack balance in their personal lives.

Achieving success in America is a real possibility. This country has always been a land of opportunity with a culture that offers success to those who take it. There are some cultures around the world that stigmatize failure. In America, failure is common. In fact, most successful entrepreneurs failed at many things before striking it rich.

This book is about finding success, and not just any kind of success. I'm talking about good success – success that combines wealth with other great benefits like health, happiness and solid family relationships.

There are countless examples of people who have achieved financial success at the expense of everything else. There are those who struggle with balancing their lives. The wealthy executive who lives in the lap of luxury whose kids won't speak to him. The preacher whose own kids are terrors. The business owner who works 70 hours a week to keep his doors open.

I recently had the privilege of traveling to Peru to do some mission work. I was amazed at the poverty I encountered. Yet the people I worked with did not consider their lives to be stressful. One of the Peruvian men with whom I traveled told me that he had grown up very poor. He came to the United States 25 years ago and became a successful businessman. He never understood what stress was until he came to our country. Even though he and many of his fellow Peruvians grew up in homes with dirt floors, they had food to eat. They interacted with their families and enjoyed outdoor activities with their friends and neighbors. In short, they were content! At that point I wondered if they should be helping us!

Some time ago, I heard a preacher suggest a solution to worrying. He said you should worry every day between noon and twelve-thirty.

If a worry pops up, remind yourself to think about it at noon. If you limit your worrying, you're on your way to experiencing good success.

The men and women who contributed ideas for this book come from all backgrounds. They come in all shapes and sizes and have different personalities. Good success does not come from following one specific program or subscribing to one specific formula. It starts with your attitude. I'm sure you've heard it said that your attitude determines your altitude. It's true! Combine a positive attitude with hard work and discipline, and I believe you can achieve greatness.

First, start by recognizing that your reality can be changed. You have the power to shape your future. It is possible to teach an old dog new tricks. Success can't begin until you're willing to believe that you can change.

Second, start observing your own negative tendencies, beliefs and affirmations. Bad habits and negative thinking will get you nothing but drama, pain and stress. Somebody once said that small-minded people talk about people, average-minded people talk about things while high-minded people talk about ideas. Watch what you talk about, what you think about and what you read and hear. There's a Bible passage in Philippians that says, "Whatsoever things are true, whatsoever things are honest, whatsoever things are just, whatsoever things are pure, whatsoever things are lovely, whatsoever things are of a good report; if there be any virtue, and if there be any praise, think on these things."

Third, have fun! Enjoy life. Get excited about the fact that you live in the greatest, most affluent country on earth! No other country gives its citizens the opportunity to succeed like America. Change the beliefs you have about your life. Set some new goals. Embrace success!

I love this quote: "When you master the art of living, there will no longer be any difference between your family time, your work and your play. You will even forget yourself if you are working or playing because you will do everything in life with so much love, fun, gusto and passion that work and play will become one. This is living."

Each of the following words came up in my conversations with successful entrepreneurs. Success is a result of combination of factors, but each person with whom I spoke said there was one factor that contributed more than anything to his or her success. Let's take a look at the 40 words and the number of people who said the word, if more than one.

Persistence – 10	Service
Consistency – 7	Dedication
Belief – 6	Attitude
Work – 6	Stick-to-itiveness
Determination – 5	Compartmentalization
Focus – 5	People Building
Vision – 4	Heart
Discipline – 3	Courage
Commitment – 2	Humor
Enthusiasm – 2	Tenacity
Passion – 2	Empathy
Desire – 2	Stability
Choices	Relationships
Dreams	Resolve
Purpose	Confidence
Energy	Passionate
Motion	Patience
Follow-up	Decisiveness
Clarity	Provision
Selflessness	Faith

PERSISTENCE

10 of 75 people that I interviewed said persistence was the most important factor in their success. I would be hard pressed to disagree. Persistence has been important in my own successes. I was a basketball player in high school. I was selected to the All-state team when I was a senior. How did I accomplish that? I practiced four hours a day, three hundred sixty days a year for seven straight years. In *Outliers*, a recent book by Malcolm Gladwell, he discusses the 10,000-hour rule – that somebody who practices a certain activity for 10,000 hours will become proficient and successful in that endeavor. For example, before the Beatles became famous they made five trips to Germany. During these extended stays they would often play gigs every night that lasted as long as 10 hours. They honed their skills during these marathon concerts.

A friend of mine had the opportunity to share a couple of drinks with Jerry Seinfeld one night. Jerry told him that he was no different than a million other comedians except for one thing. He was on a never-ending quest for success and nobody was going to stop him. He told the story of how he took a trip from New York to Texas just to be able to perform at a club for $75. It was a money losing proposition, but at that time he was willing to take any job he could get, just to perfect his skills. That attitude certainly paid off for him.

I own a carpet cleaning and water damage restoration business. One of my strategies for getting the restoration part of my business rolling was to have plumbers call me when they did work at places that had suffered water damage. There is a large plumbing company in our city that has 15 trucks. I knew we could work together, so I went to their office and asked to speak to the boss. He was unavailable, but I left him some information about my company and asked the receptionist to have him call me.

After not hearing anything for a week, I went back to his office and gave the boss's secretary a $100 gift certificate to a five-star restaurant. I instructed her to give it to him and asked again that he call me. Another week passed and I still did not hear back from him. I returned a third time. This time I gave the receptionist her own $100 gift certificate to the same restaurant and asked her to have her boss call me.

Another week passed, and still no call! I was determined to get the owner of this company to call me. My next strategy was to find one of his plumbers and offer him a $100 gift certificate if he could get his boss to call me. I happened to run into one of his plumbers at a job site and told him the gift certificate was his if he could get his boss to call me. The plumber seemed excited about the prospect. He called me back a week later to see if his boss had called me. I told him he hadn't.

Finally, two months and three $100 gift certificates later, the boss finally called me back. We had a great conversation. When I asked him why it had taken so long to return my call, he simply said that he was busy. His company now works with mine and he has sent me thousands of dollars of work. By the way, each of their plumbers gets $250 cash when a job is referred my way.

The moral to the story is simple: Don't quit! I was not going to give up the chance to speak to the owner of the plumbing company until he called me back to talk business or told me to get lost. When I tell this story to my coaching clients or people in my industry, I always end by explaining that I was not discouraged in the least by the amount of time it took for this man to call me back. I knew that if it was this hard to get this company to refer business to us, I wouldn't have to worry about my competition getting referrals. It was unlikely my competition would be as persistent as I was.

Before continuing with the next chapter, I'd like you to complete a simple task. It will be the first step on your road to success. Write down five goals you would like to achieve. These five goals can be anything you want to accomplish. You may want to achieve them this week, this year or ten years from now. The important thing is to write them down and put them where they can be seen. Which five goals pop into your head? Write them down now. It has been theorized that up to 85% of the goals you write down come to fruition. Next, put them where you can see them every day. Tape them on your bathroom mirror. Stick them to your refrigerator. Create a goal poster that you can hang in your office. It's OK if other people see your goals. In fact, you should announce them to your friends and family. Five goals to revolutionize your life! Have fun and dream big. Ask yourself if you will be willing to persist in seeing them come true. Will you? Really?

Please use the space below to write your five goals.

My Five Goals:

_____

_____

_____

_____

_____

Persistence is the mind-set of winners. No wonder it's the word most frequently mentioned when speaking of success.

"Money grows on the tree of persistence."

~ Japanese Proverb

Consistency

Yogi Berra once said, "Their similarities are different." Persistence and consistency are similar, yet different. A sales consultant who holds five appointments every week will be more successful than one who holds an appointment every now and then. The music student that practices every day will outperform the student who practices only when he feels like it. The golfer who hits 500 practice balls every day will have a greater chance of winning than the golfer who plays once a month. Naturally, the likelihood of consistent activity goes up dramatically when the activity is enjoyable. Sometimes, however, we are forced to do things we don't enjoy in order to achieve success.

A person who wants to lose weight will have to consistently stay away from eating the wrong types of food. That same person might have to consistently hit the gym whether he likes to work out or not.

Winners keep plugging away by developing good habits that bring success and happiness. If you repeat an activity for 21 days in a row, it will become a habit – either good or bad.

I have consistently marketed to realtors in my carpet cleaning business and our company receives two to five realtor referral jobs every single day. For ten years I have been going to realtor meetings and banquets. I also sponsor classes for them. In that time, I have seen many competing carpet cleaning companies attempt to get realtor referrals, but the other cleaning companies stay around for a few months and then disappear. Consistency is the key.

Now that you have listed five goals that you want to achieve, let's look at them again with the idea that you are going to consistently practice behaviors that will help you achieve them. Examine each of the five goals and ask yourself, "Am I willing to consistently work on this goal?" If, for example, your goal is to increase sales of your product or service, are you willing to talk to new prospects every day? If you want happier, engaged employees are you willing to meet with them every morning for ten to twenty minutes?

Whatever roadblocks get in your way, decide right now that you will not be stopped. You are going to do whatever it takes to make your goals and dreams come true. You will be consistent in your desire to see your dreams come true! Winners are consistent in their quest for greatness.

"For changes to be of any true value, they've got to be lasting and consistent."

~ Tony Robbins

BELIEF

Do you believe in yourself? Are you haunted by your past? Are you worried about failure? Are you afraid of success? These are common feelings, but they can be changed. In fact, they must be changed if you want to become successful.

Author T. Harv Eker has written a wonderful book called *Secrets of the Millionaire Mind* that deals with self-sabotage and other ways of thinking that will prohibit your success. I would suggest reading this book and adding it to your library.

Two people can look at the same situation and have two completely different views. For example, let's say John and Bob have businesses that are similar in size, sales volume, employees, profit, etc. Sales are OK. The bills are being paid. Nothing spectacular is going on but others in the same business are suffering. All things considered, things are going pretty well. John's thinking goes like this: "Business is good right now, and we are poised for growth. My employees are all right, but we are going to turn them into top performers. My marketing team is gaining a foothold and we are going to turn things up a notch and take off. I'm excited about our prospects and can't wait to see things explode!"

Bob thinks like this: "Business is stagnant and could be getting worse. My employees are average, but they're better than nothing. I hope they don't all quit. My marketing doesn't seem to be working. I may need to try some different forms of advertising. I just can't seem to get ahead; I really don't like this job and I'm ready to quit." Two completely different beliefs concerning the same identical situation! Which of the two men do you think has the better chance of succeeding? Is belief important? You bet it is!

Many of the entrepreneurs I interviewed talked about it. Howard Partridge, a friend of mine in the carpet cleaning industry, recently talked to me about why some people succeed and others don't. It often comes down to belief – belief in themselves, belief in their product, belief in their opportunity and belief that they deserve success.

If you're a victim of your own negative thinking, you can change! It doesn't matter what's happened in your past or who may have had a negative influence on your ability to choose success. I would suggest reading as many positive books as you can. Motivational books like *Think and Grow Rich* by Napoleon Hill or any number of books by authors like Brian Tracy, Zig Ziglar and Dale Carnegie are invaluable. You'll come to understand that there is a world out there ready to be conquered.

God designed and created you to achieve success in this world. Remember Michelangelo's comment when asked about the marble statues he created? He said he believed the figures were in the block of marble all the time just waiting to get out. I believe that you can become successful if you choose to.

Belief in your eventual success is critical to getting you started on that road to success. Do you believe the five goals you wrote down earlier can be achieved? If not, ask yourself why. If your belief wavers, share those goals with those who will encourage you and build you up.

Goals, by the way, should be specific, measurable, attainable, reasonable and time sensitive.

"You can have anything you want as long as you give up the thought that you can't have it."

~ Dr. Robert Anthony

WORK

There is no substitute for hard work! It's easier to work hard when you love what you do. My hope for you is that you love whatever career you've chosen to pursue. If you are a business owner, you know what it's like to work hard. 50, 60, 70-hour workweeks are not uncommon in order to move your business forward. Most successful business owners will tell you there's no other way. As you determine what you want to achieve, you will have to factor in the amount of time it will take you to get there. There's simply no other way.

I'm able to take a lot of vacations, but I paid my dues. Prior to owning and running a carpet cleaning business, I owned an organic bakery in Madison, WI, for 14 years. It was one of the first organic bakeries in the country and we had a good business going. We sold our goods to Chicago area health food stores. We sold via mail order and were regulars at local farmers' markets and area co-ops. Our specialty was organic whole-wheat bread made with raw, unfiltered apple cider. It tasted great, and the apple cider acted as a natural preservative. Along with the bread we made 75 other products.

During the first few years of the business I worked my tail off. I baked, bagged and delivered our bread. I would get up at 4 a.m. every day and work until 5 p.m. As the years went by I hired some additional employees and my workload decreased. I managed the business and delegated most of the day-to-day operations. Even though I put in long hours, I made a conscious effort to be at home in the late afternoon to enjoy time with my wife and my daughter. I'm sure I could have made more money had I worked longer hours, but I did not want to sacrifice the time I took to develop the two most important relationships I had in the world. I ran the bakery for 15 years before selling it for a decent profit.

We moved to Pensacola, FL, in 1990 where I opened up a carpet cleaning business. I chose the same path while building that business. I balanced my work life with my family life and the efforts have paid on both the business and family side. My business is successful and growing. On top of that, my 34-year-old daughter and her husband have moved to the Pensacola area to be near us. They have a wonderful son and beautiful baby girl.

Balancing work and family time is not always easy, but it is possible. Using your family as an excuse for failure doesn't hold water in my book. Sacrificing your family life for success in business is just as bad.

Hard work is critical for success. Efficient hard work is even better. Ever wonder why you get so much accomplished the day before you leave on a trip? It's because you're focused on accomplishing as much as possible in a short period of time. There are so many time wasting distractions available to us today. I hope that you exhibit perspicacious judgment! If you work hard and efficiently, you'll have more time to pursue leisure activities outside your business life.

"Work spares us from three evils; boredom, vice and need."

~ Voltaire

DETERMINATION

You've set five goals you want to achieve and have steered a course toward success. Now is where determination sets in. An athlete who is not determined to be the best or determined to win will not be the best and will not win. When you wake up in the morning, what do you think about? Are you determined to accomplish those things that will bring success?

When my wife began her career in direct sales she would occasionally ask me if it bothered me that she thought about her business all the time. My response? I told her it was perfectly normal for her to think about her business all the time. I knew from experience that starting and running a successful business can be an all-consuming proposition. Frankly, I had fun watching her enjoy the thrill of starting a business and pursuing her dreams. I didn't mind making my own meals or babysitting more often. I understood what she was going through because I had been the same way.

How determined are you to achieve your goals? What's your 'why'? Why do you want to achieve entrepreneurial success? Do you want to be your own boss? Would you like to quit one of the part-time jobs you have to work to make ends meet? Would you like to be able to take your family on a nice vacation? Would you like a bigger home? Understanding your 'why' will help you focus your determination on accomplishing what you set out to do. Look at your five goals one more time and ask yourself, "Am I determined to accomplish each of them?"

"An invincible determination can accomplish almost anything and in this lies the great distinction between great men and little men."

~ Thomas Fuller

Focus

Webster Dictionary defines 'focus' like this: To concentrate, as to focus one's attention. One of the concerns I have with my coaching clients is a problem that I term 'chasing rabbits.' Chasing rabbits is a common problem for business owners. It simply means they jump from one task to another without seeming to get any of them finished.

Just as a camera lens must be adjusted to clearly see an object, entrepreneurs have to focus attention on each undertaking and see each through to its conclusion. Goal setting, once again, is fundamental to this objective. Let me share with you a simple method I use to review my goals on a daily basis. I discovered this method some 25 years ago while running my bakery. It came to me at an opportune time in my bakery business. I was trying to decide whether to pay a consulting company $15,000 to come in and help me with my business. I really didn't have the $15,000, but I figured there might be a way I could get it if I really thought the consultant could help me. The company's representative was in my office waiting for me to make a decision. I was out front bagging bread. I was listening to a radio station where a man was telling a story about a business consultant that worked with large corporations. The consultant in the story had been analyzing a specific corporation for three months and was ready to present his findings to the CEO.

The CEO asked the consultant what recommendations he had for his company. The consultant told the CEO to take out a letter size piece of paper and draw two vertical lines dividing the paper into three columns.

The first column was for tasks that must be done immediately. The second column was for tasks that could wait a bit. The third column was for items that you will want to get to eventually. This column will insure that you don't forget about them.

He told the CEO to go back to the first column and prioritize the items he had listed there. The consultant then told the CEO that he should address the first item on the list and not worry about the second item until the first item was completed. The CEO's response was surprising. He handed the consultant a check for $250,000 and thanked him for what he considered invaluable advice.

The advice was profound in its simplicity and I had my answer. I went back to my office and told the consultant that I would not need his services. So, congratulations, readers! You just saved yourself a lot of money and have gotten some sound advice that you can put into practice immediately.

NASA trains some of its teams by giving them a problem and then telling them to solve it. There is no time frame for the solution. It could be hours, days, weeks, months or even years. Of course, in their line of work a quick solution can save peoples' lives. The point is that each problem has a solution. The key is to stay focused on the problem until a solution is discovered.

I still use the three-column system every day. Every evening I go to my computer and bring up 'tasks' from my documents, put tomorrow's date on it and adjust the entries on the chart. When you modify the tasks on the chart in the evening, you are the employer. When you get up in the morning to take a look at them while planning your day, you become the employee.

How focused are you? Are your goals clearly set in your mind? Have you identified and prioritized the tasks you need to accomplish to create success? Focus!

> **"Most people have no idea of the giant capacity we can immediately command when we focus all our resources on mastering a single area of our lives."**
>
> *~ Tony Robbins*

VISION

Do you have a vision for your life, your business or career? If you own your own business, do your team members share your vision? Can you visualize you and your business going places and achieving success?

My dad used to tell me that life was a lot like golf. As a lifelong golfer, I can attest to that. Professional golfers have an amazing ability to visualize shots before they hit them. Pros that can't master this skill probably won't last very long on tour.

Can you visualize your life being a good success a year down the road? Five years? Ten years? Visualization can play an important role in your dealings with customers. When a customer approaches you, can you visualize him thinking, "I'm going to like what he says. I am interested in what he has to sell." If you approach a customer thinking that he doesn't want to deal with you or purchase your product, it will show in your countenance. On the other hand, if you think they are going to love what you say, that will show in your face as well. Visualize each customer loving what you say. If you believe in your product or service it's easy to visualize customers loving what you have to offer.

Successful people are visionaries. There's a great story about an old man who asked a young boy what he saw when he looked at an acorn. The boy thought he had a wise answer when he told the old man that he saw a big, beautiful oak tree.

Well, the old man was a man of vision. He told the boy that he saw more than a tree and more than a whole forest. He saw homes and buildings and communities that had been built from that small acorn. Thomas Edison was fond of saying, "If we did all the things we are capable of doing, we would literally astound ourselves."

Take a moment to visualize what your life would like if you were able to make your goals reality. What would your house look like? What would your relationships be like? What kind of car would you drive? Where would you vacation? What would your work life be like?

Feels pretty good, doesn't it? Enjoy that feeling and affirm it regularly. An affirmation, by the way, is a statement that you make about your life where you state things as if they have already come true. Instead of saying, "I would like to make $200,000 a year," you would say, "I make $200,000 a year." Even if it's not yet a reality, you are affirming that it will be.

Olympic athletes spend countless hours visualizing themselves standing on the victor's podium listening to the playing of their country's national anthem. My wife and I put affirmations on our bathroom mirrors so we see them every day, and we say them out loud as often as possible. When we say them, we say them with belief, and so should you. It's a powerful way to build confidence in the vision you have for your life. Cut out a picture of the house you'd like to live in or vacation spots you'd like to visit. Put them on poster board and place them around your house so you see them all the time. Others may see them and think you're crazy, but that's all right. Years ago, my wife cut out a picture of a beautiful house on Pensacola Beach and taped it to our refrigerator. One day there was an open house at that home on the beach. We went to look at it even though we knew we couldn't afford it at the time. Funny how things turned out. 12 years later that same house is right across the street from where we live today! My wife has a cute sign on the front of our house that says, "Fairy Tales Do Come True."

One result of being a visionary thinker and believing in your dreams is that it comes as no surprise when your dreams come true. Now that's the way to live!

"Vision is the art of seeing what is invisible to others."

~ Jonathan Swift

DISCIPLINE

Nobody gets to the top without discipline. How do you discipline yourself? I guess the word determination comes into play. Discipline involves leaving your comfort zone. I learned discipline as a young boy when I began to understand that I had the potential to be a good basketball player. When I was in sixth grade I was only 5'4". I figured I would always be small and would have to play guard. I started practicing my ball-handling skills so I could dribble with both hands. I set up a routine where I'd dribble up and down the court with my left hand for a half hour each day. It wasn't much fun. The other kids laughed at me, but I did it anyway.

The discipline it took for me to practice paid off. Eventually I was recognized as an All-Ohio player and held a number of records at my high school for years. When I was guarded, my opponents never knew which direction I would go. I actually preferred going to my left because of all the time I had spent practicing left-handed dribbling. Fortunately, I also shot up in height. I grew from 5'4" in seventh grade to 6'1" in eighth grade. It's pretty funny to look at the little boy in the first row of my seventh-grade class picture and compare him to the third tallest boy in the top row of my eighth-grade class.

Discipline is a trait that turns most people off. When you look at your five goals, ask yourself if you are willing to discipline yourself to make them happen. Don't lie to yourself or take shortcuts. Are you willing to step outside your comfort zone and start making things happen?

Your goals might include losing weight, quitting smoking, eating healthier or getting up earlier. If so, you will have to practice discipline to make them happen. Did you know that when you accomplish a task or achieve a goal, endorphins are released into your system giving you a natural high? Imagine getting hooked on the feeling of success!

"Discipline is the bridge between goals and accomplishment."

~ Jim Rohn

COMMITMENT

Do you have a 'why'? Is there a motivating factor in your life that will propel you toward success? I can guarantee that you will have roadblocks and disappointments in your life. The ups and downs of any business are enough to test the strongest person's commitment to achieving goals.

There are countless stories of immigrants who came to this country with little or nothing but the clothes on their backs. Still, many of them became successful. They realized that opportunities in the United States were bigger and better than anything they had known before and they became committed to achieving the American dream.

I've always liked the story about the Spanish conqueror Hernando Cortez who, when his entourage landed in Mexico, burned his ships so that a return to Spain was out of the question. Now that's commitment!

There are times when you will have to stop and ask yourself a simple question: Am I committed to what I'm doing? These days commitment is a rare commodity. A marriage vow isn't what it used to be. Promises from company leaders to their workers are often broken. The 'why' of your commitment has a lot to do with your degree of allegiance. Obviously, Cortez was committed to his country and his king or maybe he just had an enormous ego. In any case, his commitment was unmistakable.

As I look back on the businesses I owned and managed, I was committed to the success of each. In the case of my bakery and restaurant, I was committed to its success, not only because it paid the bills but also because I believed in the products I was selling. The same is true for my carpet cleaning/restoration business. I believe strongly in the services we provide to our customers.

Vince Lombardi, the legendary coach of the Green Bay Packers, used to open training camp every year by holding up a football and saying, "Gentlemen, this is a football." His point was to remind his players that even though professional football at times could be very complicated, the fundamentals of the sport never changed and were paramount to success.

It's easy to make things more complicated than necessary. Whenever you entertain thoughts of giving up on your goals and dreams, remember your 'why' and get back on track.

"Unless commitment is made, there are only promises and hopes...but no plans."

~ Peter Drucker

ENTHUSIASM

If you are an entrepreneur, your clients, employees and even your vendors will want to do business with someone who is enthusiastic.

Enthusiasm is the fizz in the soda, the sizzle in the steak. Enthusiastic people are fun to be around. I believe it's possible to find success just through enthusiasm! One of the first employees in my carpet cleaning business was less than enthusiastic. I remember making a print ad for a newspaper one day. He and I were at the photographer's studio posing for a picture. The photographer asked us to give a big smile. He literally could not do it. No matter how many jokes the photographer told, he couldn't get my employee to smile.

Later on I discovered this employee had suffered through some health problems that he had sustained while in the military. His condition made it difficult for him to sleep more than three hours a night. My thought was that it would be difficult for him to be a successful business owner partly because it was next to impossible for him to act enthusiastically.

By nature, my wife is an enthusiastic person, but strategizing and planning are not her strongest assets. Nonetheless, she is very successful. I attended one of her business functions and listened to another woman in my wife's company speak. She was a dynamic speaker and very entertaining. After the event, I asked her how much time she spent preparing her presentation. She laughed and told me that she did not do a lot of planning before she spoke. She said her success was based more on her energy and enthusiasm for what she did.

I'm not saying that it's always the best course of action to forego planning and preparing, but enthusiasm can take you a long way if you channel it in the right direction. When you combine strategic planning with natural enthusiasm for what you do, great things can happen.

"Flaming enthusiasm, backed up by horse sense and persistence, is the quality that most frequently makes for success."

~ Dale Carnegie

PASSION

Passion is a first cousin to enthusiasm, but there is a difference. Passion can keep you up at night or wake you early in the morning. It gives you the drive and energy to persist when you really should be spent. Donald Trump is famous for the passion he displays when talking about his many business ventures. He rarely takes vacations because he loves his work so much. His attitude? Why take vacations when you love what you do every day?

If you own your own business, make a list of the things you don't like about it. Then make a plan of action to correct those things. Imagine what life would be like if all the negatives could be removed. It's possible to have passion for something and then lose it. If you feel that your passion for success has disappeared, take steps to reclaim it. Talk to a business coach. Sometimes a person from outside your business can see more easily things that need to be changed. Once you've identified them, start addressing the items on your list that make you unhappy. It's possible you've lost passion for other areas of your life as well.

I would suggest taking a quick test to examine your passion. Here's a simple one: List ten qualities or values that are important to you. They could be integrity, discipline, security, faith, etc. After you have ten, shorten the list to five. From those five, select one that you want to focus on.

When I did this, the word that remained from my original ten was 'passion.' The word signifies living life to its fullest, and that's what I want to do. Go back to the five goals you wrote down originally. Think about how passionate you can and will be about each of them.

"Live with passion! Passion is the genius of genius."

~ Tony Robbins

DESIRE

Some people can go through life without desiring much, while others are not satisfied until they have achieved everything they set out to do. Why is that? I understand that not everybody wants to own a large company, but I believe that everybody desires some measure of success. What desires do you have?

I was talking to a small business owner some time ago. He and his wife had decided to sell their business and go to Africa to serve as missionaries. His desires had changed pretty dramatically. I wasn't about to question him just because his passion had changed. I was happy for him. He and his wife were off to do what they really wanted to do.

Remember, your desires, like your goals, must be specific, measurable, attainable, reasonable and time specific. It's easy to compare yourself to others, yet that can be a dangerous thing to do. Each person's situation is unique. It's up to you to determine your own dreams and goals, make a plan to achieve them and then focus your desire on making them come true. Once you are focused on your own personal mission, the chance of success becomes much greater.

"Desire is the starting point of all achievement, not a hope, not a wish, but a keen pulsating desire that transcends everything."

~ Napoleon Hill

CHOICES

What a powerful and meaningful word! In America we are blessed to have so many choices available to us. When I see things like people suing fast food companies because their food is unhealthy, I have to wonder about their judgment. Why not simply choose to eat somewhere else? Sometimes I even appreciate the fact that there are bad choices available to us. It makes good choices all the more important.

People in many countries around the world live in stark poverty. On one of my trips to Peru I asked a group of teenagers if any of them wanted to grow up to be a doctors or lawyers. Not a single hand was raised. Later that evening, the Peruvian pastor with whom I was working told me the young people in his community don't think that way. Their parents probably wash windows, clean homes or pick up garbage for a living. Consequently, the young in that country assume that menial labor is the only option they will ever have. They know nothing different.

I'm personally grateful for the multitude of choices that I've had available to me all my life. Choice is something that we should celebrate. When it comes to building a successful business, there are often a lot of tough choices to be made. These choices often involve short-term sacrifice made in an effort to enjoy long-term gain.

If your business is struggling, do you choose to use your free time to complain and perform useless busywork or do you step out of your comfort zone to try some new marketing techniques? Do you allow under-performing employees to drive you crazy or do you go through the pain of finding, hiring and training new employees? Do you choose the time to make specific plans about your next quarter of business or do you just go along with the status quo and hope for the best?

I made what many considered a big mistake by dropping out of college. I had grown tired of studying and felt that the long-term gains from getting a good education were not worth the short-term sacrifices. I paid the price for that decision as a broke twenty-something employee looking to get by. I feel I rectified the situation by going into business for myself when I opened my bakery, but it took some time for me to figure out how to get ahead.

There are innumerable stories of American millionaires who did not finish college or even high school. George Bernard Shaw said that progress in the world is made by unreasonable people. Bill Gates and Paul Allen dropped out of college to start a software company called Microsoft. They spent the first years of their careers living at the office and sleeping under their desks. They made a lot of difficult decisions, but most people would agree they paid off in a big way.

What choices are you going to make next week? Are you going to choose to be proactive and determine what has to be accomplished to move you toward success, or are you going to continue to be reactive and let circumstances dictate your activities? Life is a series of daily choices. What are you going to choose?

There is a huge difference between barriers and excuses. Barriers are real obstacles that must be dealt with and overcome. Excuses, on the other hand, may be nothing more than fantasy based on fear and illusion rather than fact. If you make some bad choices, you can always pick yourself up and try again. Make choices today and tomorrow and next week that will bring you closer to achieving your five goals.

"It was a high counsel that I once heard given to a young person, 'Always what you are afraid to do'."

~ Ralph Waldo Emerson

DREAMS

In his book *The E-Myth Revisited*, author Michael Gerber emphasizes the point that each of us was made in the image of God and ought to do big things. Quite simply, the world is a mess and it needs your help. You don't have to cure cancer, but you could provide jobs for parents to bless their families. You could build a business that would allow your own children to attend good colleges and travel the world.

98% of the world's students have the brainpower to learn what is necessary to compete in this global economy. Your personal IQ should not be holding you back. Your dream IQ, however, might be another matter. Big dreams yield big results. Unfortunately, most people don't know how to dream big.

There are four levels at which people dream:

1. The first level is where things just happen to you and you have no control over them.
2. On the second level, you understand that you have control over what happens to you and that dreams do indeed have the potential to come true.
3. On the third level, dreams become a big part of your life and you put a plan of action into place to make them come true.
4. At this level you understand and believe that everything happens to you for a good reason and that your dreams will come true.

Do you have a dream that is a driving force in your life? Maybe these dreams have taken the form of a bucket list – those things that you would like to do before you die. My wife and I have a bucket list and recently added a new item. A couple that we know joined 30 other couples who chartered a Boeing 767, hired a professor to serve as a tour guide and flew around the world. They made stops in Europe, India, Asia, Australia and other points in between. The trip lasted for a month and cost each person $40,000. It's a huge dream, but it's something that my wife and I are planning to do some day. We expect it to happen!

In addition to the five goals you wrote down earlier, I'd also encourage you to write down five audacious dreams that you'd like to see come true in your life. It's OK if they seem ridiculous right now. Go ahead and write them in this book or put them on a goal poster.

My Five Audacious Dreams:

_____

_____

_____

_____

_____

How did that feel? Do you believe you can make those dreams come true?

One of my favorite stories comes from the actor Jim Carrey. One night back in 1990 when he was a struggling young comic trying to make his way in Los Angeles, he drove his old, beat-up Toyota to the top of a hill. While sitting there broke, looking over the lights of the city, he wrote himself a check for $10 million dollars. In the memo line he wrote, "For acting services rendered" and dated it for Thanksgiving of 1995.

He put that check in his wallet. The rest, as they say, is history. By 1995, Jim had seen the tremendous success of Ace Ventura, Pet Detective, The Mask and Liar, Liar. His fee per film at that point had escalated to $20 million. Was writing that check just a meaningless trick, or did it really set the stage for his eventual success?

Think about the amazing story that you can write about your own life. It's about time you got started!

> **"Coming from a small town, it was tough to dream big.
> When I grew up in a small town in Georgia, my biggest dream
> was to be able to go to Atlanta."**
>
> *~ Hershel Walker*

PURPOSE

When you look at the reasons for doing what you want to do, I hope you find one reason that is bigger than yourself! Unlike creatures in the animal world that merely exist, you have ideals and values. God made you not just to exist without purpose but also to have influence and significance. Your success will not only benefit yourself but many other people along the way.

When your life is connected to a cause greater than yourself, it's more likely you will succeed in business. I asked a hedge fund manager why he continues to work when he already makes $100 million dollars a year. He said he enjoys watching his employees making good money as well. He enjoys their success as much as his own.

Alfred Nobel, the inventor of dynamite, changed his life after mistakenly seeing his own obituary in the newspaper. His brother had died and the paper printed the wrong obituary. The writer of the obituary told how he had invented dynamite, which led to death and destruction. Alfred Nobel went ahead and donated millions of dollars to fund beneficial causes and also set up the Nobel Prize fund to recognize great achievement in various fields.

So far in this book I've asked you to determine five goals, write down five dreams and consider the path on which your life is going. I'd also like you to examine what you consider to be your purpose in life. In fact, I'd suggest writing down what you consider to be five purposes.

My Five Purposes:

_____

_____

_____

_____

_____

I've enjoyed watching my wife as her career in direct sales has unfolded. We have been blessed beyond measure because of her efforts. Free company cars, amazing trips around the world, a great income and more. Even better than those things, however, has been the positive influence she's had on our family and me and the influence she's had on other women entrepreneurs. My wife's purpose burns inside her and has brought her opportunities that we never thought existed.

I have a friend in the Czech Republic named Ludvik. He's a writer, musician and cartoonist – the quintessential Renaissance man. I met him in Berlin in 1971 when I was a student there. He was teaching art at the Free University. The German authorities allowed him to teach at the college level even though he had no degree. He was that talented. Ludvik had served six years in a Russian prison for smuggling people out of communist Czechoslovakia. Because of what he had been through, his health was somewhat fragile. However, his spirit was strong and vibrant. He loved life! When we would enter a restaurant he would disappear for half an hour. He would circulate through the restaurant greeting people, asking their opinions on what was good to eat.

During our conversation, I asked Ludvik, "How does a person like you come up with stories to write about?"

Ludvik looked me in the eye and said, "My friend, I don't create them. They are already out there in the universe, and they come to me!"

There is a purpose in the universe for you to fulfill. When you find it, act on it! Your life will be enriched beyond measure.

"The purpose of human life and the sense of happiness is to give the maximum that the person is able to give."

~ Alexander Alekhine

ENERGY

A man who happens to be a Dale Carnegie franchisee owner for over 30 years submitted the term energy to my study. He personifies energy! Without personal energy, it's difficult to accomplish the every day tasks necessary to achieve success. Even though people have accomplished great things despite ill health, I know in my life it has always been easier to work hard and pursue success when I feel good.

While in Peru, I asked the man with whom I was staying about the main causes of death in his country. He thought for a bit and then told me it was car accidents. I had been witness to the crazy driving habits of the Peruvian people, so I was not surprised. However, I still asked, "Don't people die of cancer?"

He said, "Not really." He went on to tell me that there was only one cancer hospital in the entire country. I asked if people died of heart attacks. Again, he told me that not many people died that way either for the simple reason that the Peruvian diet is simple. They eat grains, beans and vegetables and the stress level is generally low.

Quite a contrary picture in our country. If you're like the average American who eats an overabundance of processed or fast foods that are high in sugar and fat, you more than likely will face some challenges when it comes to maintaining peak energy.

In order to work hard, you need energy. In order to maintain energy, you need to eat a proper diet, get plenty of exercise and enough sleep.

These are choices that you can make that will have a great impact on your ability to be successful.

"Passion is energy. Feel the power that comes from focusing on what excites you."

~ Oprah Winfrey

MOTION

Business is rarely static; your business never stands still. You are either gaining momentum or losing it.

Top athletes understand this concept better than most. They can't afford to take much time off or skills will diminish and competitors will pass them by. The business scene in America is no different. There is a tremendous amount of competition out there. If you rest on your laurels, others will pass you by.

Bill Gates has a simple formula for success: Be in the right industry at the right time and take massive action.

If I could add anything to that concept, it would be the following: TO BE SUCCESSFUL, KEEP TAKING MASSIVE ACTION!

Staying in motion includes a variety of tactics. Continue improving your business systems. Keep tweaking your marketing strategies. Keep building your bottom line. One of my neighbors is a successful business-man. He owns three other homes and rarely stays in Pensacola more than two days a month. He owns a steel mill in Scotland, a plastics factory in Cleveland and 28 other businesses. When I asked him about the secret to success, he said, "Make your businesses saleable, and then don't sell."

He told me the only way to build profitable turnkey businesses is to stay in motion. Hire strong people for management positions and pay them well. He has incentive programs for his managers that are tied to each company's profitability.

When I asked him how he could possibly oversee 30 different businesses, he said it was simple. When he looks at the financial position of each company, he identifies those that are doing well and leaves them alone. When he identifies a company that is underperforming, he steps in and investigates to determine what can be done to right the ship.

Successful companies are always in motion, changing and adapting with the times. Look at AT&T, for example. Even their name is an enigma… American Telephone and Telegraph. When was the last time you sent a telegram or used a home-based landline for that matter? AT&T has been able to stay in the forefront of the telecommunications industry by embracing companies like Apple and their amazing iPhone.

Forward momentum is an amazing thing. If your business is moving forward like an athlete with a head of steam, good things will happen. If your business is starting and stopping like an airplane that continually takes off and lands, you will struggle to maintain forward momentum.

Set a course for you business and stick to it. Work each day at accomplishing your goals. Keep your momentum moving forward!

"A static hero is a public liability. Progress grows out of motion."

~ Richard C. Byrd

Follow-up

This won't appear to be an important concept for many people, but I can assure you that it is. Follow-up is crucial for success!

In the Bible Jesus told a story about a woman who goes to see an unjust judge. She wants to be avenged of her adversary. The unjust judge doesn't listen and doesn't seem to want to help her. The woman keeps pleading with the judge for him to listen. Finally, the judge rules in her favor. (Luke 18:2)

I'm not advocating being a pest, but I can assure you that many business ventures have failed because of no follow-up. For people in business arenas similar to mine or my wife's, follow-up is especially critical for the simple reason that sales transactions are based on individual appointments. There are plenty of reasons for follow-up not to occur. Poor systems, fear of rejection and bad time management are just a few.

Do you follow up with leads? Do you follow up a sale with good customer service? Do you plan to follow up with your future plans?

Staying accountable to your goals is very important. It may take external help in the form of a business coach or partner to keep you on track, but sometimes that help is necessary. I meet weekly with a business coach and I never want to feel embarrassed when I see him. He always asks me if I've done what I said I was going to do the week before. It's been great motivation for me to keep moving forward in pursuit of my dreams and goals.

Below are some startling statistics relating the effectiveness of follow-up:

- 48% of initial sales contacts are never followed up.
- 25% make two contacts.
- 12% make three contacts.
- 10% make more than three contacts.
- 2% of sales are made after the first contact.
- 3% are made after the second contact.
- 5% are made after the third contact.
- 10% are made after the fourth contact.
- 80% are made after five or more contacts!

"Follow-up the interview with a phone call. If Carrot Top can learn how to use a phone, so can you."

~ Tom Cole

CLARITY

Successful people are clear about what they want to accomplish. Are you clear about what you want to achieve? Do you have a written plan? If not, this might be a good time to work on one. I'm serious! Your plan for success should be on paper.

Do you know where you want to be in the next 90 days? How about the next six months? What about the next five years? There are some Japanese companies that have 100-year plans. That may seem crazy, but it's true.

Your plan should not just be about you. What about your children? What about the legacy you want to leave behind? Instead of a 100-year plan, why not a 500-year plan — one that takes into consideration future generations that could be affected by what you accomplish today?

My wife's 95-year-old father instilled in her the idea that you can be anything you want to be. He always encouraged her to follow her dreams, work hard, keep a positive attitude and love life. He told her to never stop learning and to enjoy each day as if it was her last. To her credit, she took his advice and has passed it on to our daughter. Our daughter now has a beautiful baby boy and girl, and guess what? She is passing those same traits down to them! Their lives will be shaped by the same concepts and ideals that shaped generations before them.

A good golfer knows that when he lines up a putt, he has to visualize in his mind which way the putt will break. Once he figures out the break, he has to commit to hitting the putt exactly where he thinks it should go. Think of your goals the same way. Are you clear where you want to go?

If there is confusion, eliminate it. Then, like a golfer hitting a solid putt, commit to your line of thinking and go for it!

"Your mind, while blessed with blessed with permanent memory, is cursed with lousy recall. Written goals provide clarity. By documenting your dreams, you must think about the process of achieving them."

~ Gary Ryan Blair

Selflessness

In your quest for success, it's not always about you. Certainly you are involved in your own quest for success. And, let's be honest, in many cases you are going to be concerned about you before anyone else. You will always try to make sure you have food to eat, clothes on your back and a roof over your head. It's possible that you have taken care of these matters above and beyond what is considered adequate and are still miserable.

It's my belief that selfish people are unhappy because they forget to do one thing – help others. Your business or career is probably designed to help other people in some way. When you put forth effort to help improve the lives of others, it will be evident in your life. If you are concerned only about yourself, it may be possible to still achieve success, but it's unlikely that you'll enjoy it.

If you're like me, you probably know some people who only talk about themselves or try to top every story you tell. Those kinds of people wear out their welcome quickly. On the other hand, you know what a pleasure it is to be around people who are others focused. They ask about you and are sincerely interested in what you have to say. I have met sales people in both categories, and I can tell you from experience that I'm more likely to buy a product from the second kind of person than the first. There have been times I've purchased items from a salesperson just because the person was nice.

Are you self-centered when you talk to others? Are you likable? Are you others focused? Will the goals you have written down help make you a better person?

"We are formed and molded by our thoughts. Those whose minds are shaped by selfless thoughts give joy when they speak or act. Joy follows them like a shadow that never leaves them."

~ Buddha

SERVICE

People who serve others are some of the happiest people I know. It's one of the reasons I've enjoyed working in a service industry. Also, I've been asked why I would leave the comforts of my country to travel on mission trips to third world countries. I always tell them the same thing. I come back from these trips a grateful, fulfilled, better person.

I have an average performing employee in my carpet cleaning business who, in my opinion, is capable of becoming a top performer. He has many good traits and clients like him, but he does exhibit some negative tendencies. One day I overheard him talking to my operations manager. He said he was tired of 'cleaning up other people's messes.' I caught the negative tone of the conversation realizing that this is the kind of vibe that can have a detrimental effect on our clients and other employees. I pulled him aside and told him that he could just as easily be saying that he loves to help people and is satisfied when he leaves a customer's home with their carpets looking great. The attitude displayed by a person with a servant's heart will be easy to spot and is valued by clients, especially in a service related business like mine.

In addition to the five goals you listed earlier, you may want to add an activity or two that are wholly service oriented. Any ideas? Let me provide one example of how a single person can make a difference in the world through serving others.

One historical figure that I really admire is the 19th-century English evangelist named John Wesley. He traveled up and down the English countryside over the course of his career. He was dismayed by the drab poverty of village life. He decided to distribute flower seeds to housewives as he traveled and have contests to see who could grow the most beautiful gardens. One of the reasons today's English countryside is known for its beauty and color goes back to the simple service that Wesley provided over a century ago.

"It has always been my belief that a man should do his best, regardless of how much he receives for his services, or the number of people he may be serving or the class of people served."

~ Napoleon Hill

DEDICATION

Most business owners are dedicated to their businesses because time and money are at stake. But the bigger question is this: Are they dedicated to success?

Are you willing to pay the price for success? Or are you just going through the motions so others will think you are dedicated? Being dedicated to success means you'll be willing to step out of your comfort zone. Being dedicated to success means you'll stay on top of industry trends. Being dedicated to success means you'll be willing to work long hours. Being dedicated to success means setting your sights high!

There will always be days when you feel like throwing in the towel. If you believe in what you are doing, however, these feelings can be overcome. If you determine that you are not dedicated to the business you're currently in, then maybe it's time to change course. Life is too short and too precious to waste it doing things that you don't like to do.

If you can look at the five goals you wrote down and dedicate yourself to achieving them, you are on the track to success.

"I know the price of success: dedication, hard work and unremitting devotion to the things you want to see happen."

~ Author Unknown

ATTITUDE

One of the most fascinating people I ever met was a Christian Ethiopian Jew. He told me of his life as a child growing up in communist Ethiopia. His grandfather had been an official in the communist government. His mother was a Christian who prayed many hours each day. The communist authorities, including his grandfather, hated the Ethiopian Jews and often times killed them when they had the opportunity. He said he had spent many nights sleeping under tables and hiding away in order to stay alive.

As a teenager, he began to read the Bible and eventually became a Christian. This made his grandfather hate him even more. He tried to emigrate to the United States but was turned down by U.S. embassy officials. He told me that once he had been turned down three times, the chance that he could get to the U.S. was gone. One morning his mother told him to go quickly to the embassy. While she had been praying, she said an angel had told her that her son would get the permission he needed to emigrate to the U.S. He listened to his mother and returned to the embassy for the fourth time. The same people who had denied his request three times before stamped his card and gave him permission to leave his country. Azaria came to the U.S., got an education and became quite wealthy in the financial services industry. He chose to use some of his wealth to do mission work in South America, the place where I eventually would meet him.

Azaria is a quiet man and would not share much, but I continued to ask him about his life. After another two hours of conversation, I returned to my hotel room and made some notes about our talk. One of his most insightful observations concerned the extreme poverty in much of South America and Africa. Both continents are blessed with abundant mineral resources yet they are extremely poor. When I questioned Azaria about this perplexing situation, he pointed to his head and said, "It's all about their attitude! The people have no dreams. They don't think about success and continue in the ways of those who have gone before them. If they realized what they had and changed their attitudes, they could rise up and live lives of prosperity and abundance."

How would you describe your attitude? Do you believe you are capable of tremendous success? Is your attitude an asset or a liability?

> **"Attitude is more important than the past, than education, than money, than circumstances, than what people say or do. It is more important than appearance, giftedness, or skill."**
>
> *~ W.C. Fields*

STICK-TO-ITIVENESS

I would like to refer to this quality as 'pit bull mentality.' If you've ever watched a dog chew on a bone, I think you know what I'm talking about. That dog is focused. He protects what he has and won't let anybody take it from him.

If your competition has this quality and you don't, who do you think will win out in the long run? If you've made the effort to purchase and read this book, I assume you are the type of person who doesn't settle for mediocrity. I assume you're the type of person who wants to go to the top. If you adopt a pit-bull mentality – a serious stick-to-itiveness – you can go to the top quicker than somebody with a so-so attitude. Are you like a dog on a bone or is your attitude best described as "come what may and it is out of my hands?"

"The three great essentials to achieve anything worthwhile are first, hard work; second, stick-to-itiveness; third, common sense."

~ Thomas Edison

Compartmentalization

This word is especially important for women entrepreneurs. Since emotions, thoughts and feelings are lumped together in the brain, it may at times be difficult separating business from personal matters, especially for women.

It seems to me, for example, that men have more difficulty finding things than women do. When I look for something in the refrigerator, I sometimes have difficulty; my wife can find what she's looking for immediately. I look in the refrigerator and have tunnel vision. My eyes only see a limited view. When my wife looks in, her vision is peripheral and she sees all over the place. Why is that? Could it be that men and women think differently? Could it be that men think more logically while women think more emotionally? Studies have shown that men's and women's brains are different.

For business owners, the ability to compartmentalize is important because they tend to live and work in the business 24 hours a day. I was talking with a coaching client recently who said he was tired all the time. He's only 41 years old, which is much too young to be tired all the time. When I asked him what he did in the evenings and on weekends, he said, "I think about work all the time."

I said, "No wonder you're tired all the time. You're literally working 18 hours a day or more!"

He needed to compartmentalize – that is, to work hard and efficiently when doing business but to relax and turn off the business when not working. I recently read a book called *When I Relax I Feel Guilty*. Do you know how to turn it off? Do you know how to relax? The Greek word for leisure is *schole*, from which we get the words school and scholar. The ancient Greeks understood the relationship between work and leisure and believed that learning ought to be fun. Hopefully your business will be the vehicle that allows you to accomplish your dreams and goals.

The thinking part of our brain should be the servant to who we are. Albert Einstein talked about our self consisting of two distinct parts. The one part is our soul, our natural unique self. The other part is our thinking, which serves who we are. Too often in this modern age, especially for business owners, the thinking part takes over and the soul becomes smaller and smaller until all that remains is our thinking. You can see it happen yourself when you try to concentrate on a given task and notice how quickly your mind begins to wander.

A teacher asked the class to stop all activity. He handed each student a raisin and asked the students to clear their minds. He told them to think about nothing except how the raisin tasted. He told them as soon as their minds wandered from the task of describing how the raisin tasted, they were to raise their hands. Within 12 seconds every hand was up.

It's difficult to live in the present. We spend so much time thinking about what could have been or what we could have done differently that we forget to enjoy each day as it is.

Of course you need to think about your business plans and strategies, but you need to be able to turn it off too. You have to take time off to watch your kids play ball, attend a concert, learn a new language, plant a garden, read a book, cook a meal or whatever it is that makes you happy outside of your work life.

In Winston Churchill's book *Why I Paint*, he talks about the fact that his mind never shut off. To help himself relax, he learned how to paint. He found that when he painted, he could forget about all the problems he was facing and live in the moment. It was soothing and relaxing for him to think about nothing but the picture he was painting.

One of my greatest joys is being with my grandson. At the time I wrote this he was 18 months old. I learn by observing him. He doesn't live in the past or worry about the future. He lives in the moment. I enjoy that and have tried to emulate him!

Take some time to analyze your schedule. How can everything fit together to give you a balanced life? Work, time with family, personal leisure time, vacation, spiritual time, time with friends, quiet time – all of these can be balanced to make your life enjoyable.

"These guys have a tremendous ability to compartmentalize – put all the junk to the side and play the game. All the other stuff they can't control. What we can control is what happened out there."

~ Coach Chan Gailey

PEOPLE BUILDING

Successful people add to the emotional bank accounts of others. They make others feel good about themselves. They are interested in improving the lives of those around them. Leadership involves building people. If you have employees, one of your jobs is to help make them better. You do this by encouraging them and providing them with concepts and skills that will help them win.

If you've ever asked yourself, "Whom should I build up?" I would suggest this answer: EVERYONE! The waitress that serves you dinner, the landscaper who mows your lawn, the clerk at the gas station, the student who babysits your children, the receptionist at the doctor's office and especially your customers. Everybody wants to feel important. A good listener looks the other person in the eye, doesn't interrupt, doesn't change the subject and responds to what the speaker is saying.

Listening is a skill. Generally in a conversation, the person who is doing the majority of the listening has the upper hand. I know it sounds counterintuitive, but you can build others up just by listening to them. And a compliment or a 'thank-you' won't hurt either!

I'd like you to think of three people right now that you could make a conscious effort to build up.

My Three People To Build Up:

_____

_____

_____

"Successful people have the ability to develop relationships that last."

~ Ray Farmer

HEART

It's not always how smart a person is, but how big that person's heart is. Heart makes a difference! When you deal with people for a living, caring about them and giving to them will be critical to your success. Jesus said, "Give and it shall be given unto you." It's almost like the law of gravity. If you want good things to come into your life you have to send good things into the lives of others. If you have a caring heart, you will be able to make the lives of others better.

It's my feeling that heart may be more important than brains when it comes to achieving success in business. Studies have shown that heart transplant patients have dramatic personality changes after their operations. It could only mean that the heart is a critical part of your personality. The organ that keeps you alive also plays a role in determining who you are.

When you look at the five goals you wrote down earlier, examine them with your head and then with your heart. How does your mind feel about them? How does your heart feel about them? You may come to realize that your heart may be more important than your head when it comes to achieving your goals.

"The greatest treasures are those invisible to the eye but found by the heart."

~ Author Unknown

COURAGE

Being the owner of a small business or being an entrepreneur in a direct selling business takes courage. One of the most famous acts of all time can be found in the Old Testament. David was a teenager when he faced the giant Goliath. That fact alone illustrates that courage is not necessarily based on age or experience. How could a young shepherd boy with no military experience face a veteran warrior who stood nearly 10 feet tall?

1. He was confident he could defeat this enemy because of past victories. David had killed a bear and a lion by himself prior to his battle with Goliath.

2. He had a defined purpose going into battle. He was angry with Goliath for insulting his God.

3. He had clarity in his approach to the fight. He took five stones with him. In case he missed with the first shot or two, he had a back up.

4. He had worked hard to prepare for this moment. As a shepherd, David had no doubt practiced with the slingshot and perfected his aim in order to protect his sheep from predators. When the time came for him to test his skill, he was ready.

5. He made sound strategic decisions. When King Saul suggested he wear heavy armor into battle, David refused. He had never worn armor before and knew it would slow him down.

Can a story like this translate to modern times? Yes! Can you make use of it in your own life? Of course you can!

When you are confident, you are more likely to be courageous. Confidence is built by winning small victories. Defeats will happen, but they can only help steel you for the battles ahead.

Having a purpose will enable you to accomplish incredible feats. Your purpose always goes back to your 'why.' A recent study looked at people who had open-heart surgery and were told they had to change their diet and living habits to avoid clogging their arteries again. Only 10% actually listened to this advice and changed their lifestyles. The study found there were three reasons people made significant changes in their lifestyles. First, they got involved in an activity that was bigger than they were. Second, they understood the impact that changes would have on the rest of their lives. Thirdly, they received help from others.

Young David certainly viewed his mission with clarity. He knew he was going to succeed in killing his enemy. Courage comes partly from the clarity you have in your mission.

Hard work and experience also shape courage. If you are just starting a business and have no experience, you can still muster courage based on the knowledge that you will be willing to make the necessary sacrifices to be successful.

Know who you are. Don't make the mistake of trying to be somebody else. You can learn from others and take ideas from others, but you have to be yourself. Set your mind on success, follow your values and it will be easier to act courageously.

Finally, don't be afraid to fail. Failure can be a great teacher. Courageous people are not afraid of failure. God doesn't give you courage; he gives you opportunities to act courageously.

"Courage is the resistance to fear, mastery of fear, not absence of fear."

~ Mark Twain

HUMOR

Humor may not be the most important ingredient for success, but it sure makes the ride a lot more fun. Laughter can conquer a host of ills. Proverbs 15:13 says that a merry heart makes a cheerful countenance. Your countenance is how you look to others. Wouldn't you prefer doing business with a person who has a bright countenance? Without using humor as a release, think of all the negative energy that is stored up inside of you.

When I spent time as an evangelist, I could often determine the spiritual condition of my listeners by telling some jokes or light-hearted stories. If the congregation couldn't laugh or enjoy themselves, I knew there were problems. People want to do business with those they enjoy being around.

By the way, let me suggest one caution when telling a joke or story to a group of people. If you wonder about the appropriateness of the joke, don't tell it. Listen to your own voice of caution in this matter and you'll save yourself some heartache down the road.

"Common sense and a sense of humor are the same thing moving at different speeds. A sense of humor is just common sense dancing."

~ William James

TENACITY

Don't quit! Never give up! Once you have made a decision, stick with it! Tenacity and persistence are similar traits. However, tenacity implies finishing the job. Successful people don't quit until a job is completed.

I learned a lesson in tenacity when I was in high school. I used to play pick-up games of basketball with friends of mine as well as some players from a rival high school. We would play games up to 100 baskets. I remember one game where we were getting beat 99-82. The other team only needed to make one more shot to win the game. We closed the score from 99-85 and finally 99-93. At this point, we began to think we might have a chance to win. We closed the gap to 99-95 having scored 13 baskets in a row. By this time we were thinking that we were going to win for sure. Our opponents were frazzled and out of sync and seemed incapable of making another shot. In the end, we came back to win the game 100-99, and I learned a lesson that I would never forget. It's never over 'til it's over!

I love the movie Rudy. It's one of the best examples of tenacity that I can think of. To see a 5'6" 165 lb. athlete walk on to play for a big time college football program is nothing short of inspiring. Each time you review your five goals, you can think about Rudy. Stay the course, and you will achieve success!

"The history of the world is full of men who rose to leadership, by sheer force of self-confidence, bravery and tenacity."

~ Mahatma Ghandi

EMPATHY

Growing up, I never heard this word. In the world in which I lived, everybody was supposed to take care of his own problems. Identifying with the problems of another person was considered a weakness.

To empathize simply means putting yourself in another's place. It is a noble thing to do in many instances. It shows you care about others and puts you in the position of being able to help.

There are few businesses that don't involve dealing with a lot of different people. If making money is your only focus, you will be missing out on an even greater payoff. That is the chance to work with and help other people.

At first, I found it a bit strange that this word even appeared on the list. However, I believe that understanding and showing empathy toward others can go a long way in turning you into a good success.

"True contentment comes with empathy."

~ Tim Flinn

STABILITY

Emotional stability can go a long way toward defining your success. It doesn't matter whether you're a male or female. Some might say the women are led more by emotion than men, but in the business world both genders will profit by maintaining emotional stability.

It's easy to let your emotions run wild, especially when you're going through hard times. When business is slow or when you have problems with an employee it's possible to get stuck on an emotional level, sometimes for a very long time. My wife tells the story of one of her business consultants who told her she had finally forgiven a person for something that had happened 30 years earlier. She had been stuck in a bitter memory about a teammate who had dropped a baton in a race back in a high school track meet. Talk about being stuck!

Emotions are part of each person's makeup, but they shouldn't control your life. There are some cases where you'll have to get your emotions under control and make decisions based on logic and positive thinking. The positive attitude that I've talked about before can go a long way towards helping you maintain emotional stability.

RELATIONSHIPS

My own wife provided this word on my list of 40. Kate has a special knack for inspiring others toward success. She has been able to get people to accomplish things they never thought possible. When you build relationships with your clients, you are putting yourself in the position to do the same things.

When I moved my carpet cleaning company into a new facility, I sponsored an open house. We served gourmet food and offered some great door prizes and exciting entertainment. It cost quite a bit, but it established our brand as one that was upscale and a cut above the rest. It helped cement relationships that already existed.

Each personal relationship that you form is unique. I would strongly recommend reading books that describe personality types so that you can better understand people. One of the most common personality profiles uses the DISC descriptions to categorize personality traits and there are many tools connected with this program to help you learn. I would suggest taking the DISC test yourself and then picking up some books that teach you how to utilize the information.

To illustrate the importance of understanding personality types, I'll share one quick story about my daughter. Kali and her husband were in a checkout line at a local hardware store when they realized they had forgotten to pick up a garden hose attachment. Josh went back to get the nozzle while Kali stayed in line. Getting somewhat irritated that it was taking so long, Kali left the line to find out what was going on. Josh's personality tends to be one of careful examination. He was having a hard time picking out a nozzle. Kali tends to be more impulsive and makes decisions quickly. When she found him, she let him know she was upset that he had taken so long. At that point, they both started laughing. They both know about personality traits and understood that this was something not worth arguing about. Josh wasn't trying to be mean; he just takes his time when buying something.

In order to be a good success, you will have to be a people builder with a true concern for developing positive relationships with others.

"The ability to deal with people is as purchasable a commodity as sugar or coffee and I will pay more for that ability than for any other under the sun."

~ John D. Rockefeller

RESOLVE

This word was supplied by one of the top earners in my wife's company. She has had commission checks in excess of $100,000 in a month. Tenacity, persistence and resolve go hand in hand. In the case of this particular woman, her resolve is always on display. I attended a convention where she spoke and it didn't even strike me as improbable when she announced to the entire crowd of 5,000 people that her goal was to earn $400,000 per month.

A person's resolve is manifested in his or her personal discipline and is what I consider to be a great component of one's character. You might look at a person who earns that much money in a month and consider them to be out of the ordinary. My contention is that resolve can be developed, especially after attempting to reach a goal, failing and then trying again until that goal is achieved.

Wouldn't you love to be viewed as a person who is full of resolve? A person who could stand on stage in front of thousands and pass that feeling on to others?

"Obstacles cannot crush me. Every obstacle yields to stern resolve. He who is fixed to a star does not change his mind."

~ Leonardo Da Vinci

CONFIDENCE

This word was supplied by one of the most successful college football coaches in the country. Confidence is as valuable in the business world as it is on the football field. Confidence will open doors for you and get you in front of decision makers.

You can't conjure up confidence out of nowhere. It comes from two sources — preparation and experience. An alliteration that I've used with my clients goes like this: Proper preparation prevents poor performance. Being prepared to meet a prospective client can give even the greenest rookie a small measure of confidence.

Most people that I know are uncomfortable speaking in public. Proper preparation can calm the nerves and make for a successful presentation.

Confidence also is a by-product of experience, especially successful experience. The phrase 'fake it 'til you make it' has some truth to it. However, there always has to be a degree of preparation so you can walk into intimidating situations with your head up and your confidence level high.

Once you have developed confidence in what you do and how you speak, you can take it to the bank — literally. I'm not talking about conceit or overconfidence. I'm talking about true confidence rooted in preparation and experience.

Confidence must be tempered by wisdom, but it's essential for good success. When the game is on the line, you should be the one looking to take the last shot. Why? Because you know you can make it.

"Confidence never comes out of nowhere. It's a result of something... hours and days and weeks and years of constant work and dedication."

~ Roger Staubach

PASSIONATE

You will be passionate about those things that you love. So, what do you love about your business or career? In my carpet cleaning business I love supervising marketing development. I love meeting new people. I love preparing and delivering speeches and presentations. I don't particularly care to answer phones, do bookwork or run a truck. One of the benefits of growth in my company is that I rarely have to do things I don't enjoy. There was a time when I had to do everything. Now I'm able to focus my energy and passion on those things that I'm best at.

How will you be able to tell what you're passionate about? Well, you can start by making a list of those things that you don't enjoy doing and go from there. When you are in the position to work the way you want, focus on those things that make you the happiest and delegate the rest.

"Find something you are passionate about and keep tremendously interested in it."

~ Julia Child

PATIENCE

It's possible that I'm not the best person in the world to teach patience. Like many other Americans, I want everything right away. Instant gratification is a way of life for most of us. Having said that, I can also promise you that patience will be a virtue in your business. Patience, if nothing else, will help you avoid costly mistakes.

I hate to even think about all the money I've wasted or lost over the years because I was impatient when making important decisions. In most cases, I failed to get good counsel or study a situation carefully enough. I can almost guarantee that you will have situations with employees, clients or customers that require patience. Successful people have a knack for pulling back and analyzing situations before plowing ahead. Successful people are able to wait for results and don't get frustrated when results don't appear as quickly as they want.

In my wife's business, it takes patience to win over new customers and bring others into the company. Practicing patience will allow other good qualities like focus and discipline to become apparent. If you want a great precept for making intelligent, patient decisions, go by the following rule. Before making a decision, ask yourself, "What is the downside to this decision." Always ask yourself that question prior to moving ahead and you may avoid many large and small mistakes.

"Patience is the companion of wisdom."

~ St. Augustine

DECISIVENESS

Every day you are faced with hundreds of decisions. One of the reasons people don't go into business for themselves is that they either can't or won't make decisions for themselves. Most entrepreneurs that I know are decision makers. They are leaders, not followers.

As the owner of multiple business ventures, I've had to make thousands, if not millions of decisions over the years. I enjoy that aspect of being a business owner. I think I would go crazy if I had to always follow other people's decisions.

I believe that being successful is a decision. Have you made that decision for yourself yet? Or are you still wondering if you can be successful? Without a firm decision in your own mind, it's unlikely that you will be highly successful. Each January 1st people all over the country make resolutions to change. Too often those resolutions are abandoned within a couple of days. Are you going to wait another year to reach success? Have you made a firm decision that this is going to be your year? I hope you have.

There have been times in my wife's business where her end goal seems unreachable to a pragmatic thinker. But she has always believed in herself, and when she sets her mind to something, it doesn't matter how far away the goal is, I have come to learn that she will do it. Her unwavering belief, combined with great work ethic, always overcame the obstacles that popped up on her road to success.

Life is never better than when you step out of your comfort zone, overcome obstacles and achieve miraculous results!

"The quality of decision is like the well-timed swoop of a falcon which enables it to strike and destroy its victim."

~ Sun Tzu

PROVISION
(PERSISTENT VISION)

Provision is a clever word to describe the concept of never taking your eye off the prize. Never forget to dream and dream big. Your goals are merely stepping-stones to achieving your dreams and you have to maintain sight of the big picture.

One of my technicians was complaining recently that he had only been able to work 30 hours during a particular week. He had forgotten that he had worked 48 and 50 hours the previous two weeks. He had lost track of the big picture and only considering the immediate situation. Had he done some simple math, he would have realized that he had averaged more than 40 hours each of the three weeks. It's easy to get stuck in that kind of short-sighted thinking. We all do it frequently. The good thing about big dreams is that small setbacks don't seem as important. By keeping track of the overall picture of your big dream, you'll be able to counter short-term thinking like this.

FAITH

One person I interviewed told me that faith was the most important component of success. If you are not a person of faith, I would still encourage you to read this final section. If nothing else, there are some simple words of wisdom from which you may benefit.

In the Old Testament book of Joshua 1:8 there is the following passage: "This book of the law shall not depart out of your mouth; but you shall meditate on it day and night, that you might do according to all that is written there. For then you shall make your way prosperous and then you shall have good success."

I like how Joshua added the word 'good' in that sentence. I have talked about good success throughout this book and it's my sincere hope for you that you find it. It's my belief that one of the reasons our country has been so successful is that it was founded on Judeo-Christian ethics and beliefs.

By following God and living a life of faith, you will hopefully make grounded decisions, avoid being self-centered and have access to a wisdom that can only come from knowledge of the Creator.

I have a short daily affirmation that I say regularly. "I pray, plan, produce, profit and play." It starts with a daily prayer for wisdom and guidance. When I have important decisions to make, I ask God for guidance. When I need help, I turn to the One who knows all things, including my future.

Finally, Proverbs 3:5-6 says, "Trust in the Lord with all your heart and lean not unto your own understanding; in all your ways acknowledge Him and He will direct your paths."

CONCLUSION

Now that you've had the chance to examine *40 Words*, my hope for you is that somewhere you will have gained something that will make a positive difference in your life. Maybe you recognized a quality that you already have and will take it to a new level. Perhaps you read about a quality that you lack and will try harder to develop it.

40 words from 75 influential people. There is no better time than right now to decide that you are ready to start living a powerful, productive, prosperous and pleasurable life.

You can have it all in this great country of ours, so why not stake your claim for greatness and happiness. The world needs you to step up to the plate and make this a better place to live. Only one question remains: When are you going to move forward? The best answer is simple: Now!

Bonus Words

Since completing this manuscript, I have continued to ask businessmen and women to tell me, in a word, what it takes to be successful. I've heard words like integrity, honesty, luck, adaptability and others. Two words struck me as profound, and I decided to include them as a bonus to the original 40 words.

FAILURE

That's right. Failure. Without question, successful people fail more often than others because they are willing to take risks. Anytime you take a risk in business there's a chance you might fail. On the other hand, successful people are willing to get back up and try again, even after failing. They don't let failure define them. The number of things they strive to accomplish defines them. Successful people have a lot on their plate; unsuccessful people usually don't.

The person who talked to me about failure knows a thing or two about this subject. He did top-secret espionage work for a foreign government. His job was to infiltrate corporations owned and operated by a hostile neighboring country and take steps to bring those companies down. Today he is a business consultant doing just the opposite kind of work. Using his knowledge of how to destroy businesses, he is helping to build businesses instead.

One of the biggest failures of all time was Thomas Edison. He had so many bad ideas and unsuccessful endeavors that in some people's eyes he would be considered a pathetic failure. Still, he probably did more to change the way you and I live than any human being in modern history.

After Edison's successful invention and development of the incandescent light bulb, many wonderful changes occurred in the daily lives of people around the world.

But listen to some of his ideas that failed: Edison thought a house could be made out of poured concrete. He would use one mold for the entire structure and pour concrete into the form in a continuous flow.

He wanted the whole house to be concrete including the doors, toilets, cabinets and even the piano. He actually designed and built a few of them, but obviously the idea never took off.

Edison also spent a significant amount of time and money to develop automated, coin-operated stores. Put a coin in the machine and out comes potatoes, a toothbrush, coal, or whatever else the customer wanted. It was a dismal failure.

In the final analysis, failure remains a component of success. It's my hope that you have plenty of failures in the future because each of them will play a part as you travel down the road to success and happiness.

"Only those that dare to fail greatly will achieve greatly."

~ Robert Kennedy

PERSPICACIOUS

This final word, perspicacious (insightful, perceptive, wise) was shared with me by another fascinating source – an astronaut. This friend of mine has been to space four times. Based on that accomplishment alone, he can be considered a tremendous success. But he also went on to become an engineer and a doctor. When I asked him to tell me in one word what it takes to be a success, he shared with me a word you don't hear every day, "Perspicacious," he said.

He went on to explain it this way. "As an astronaut and as a businessman, you have to learn how to put elements together that matter and then act on them. You can't get distracted by the noise."

I thought it was a perfect way to close this book. As a businessperson, you have to examine what is out there, decide on a course of action based on sound judgment and then take massive action! In space, an astronaut has to be perspicacious or people can die. For those in the business world the same type of sound judgment is necessary or you'll go broke.

Made in the USA
Charleston, SC
22 May 2012